Mildred Taylor

The Library of Author Biographies™

MILDRED TAYLOR

Gillian Houghton

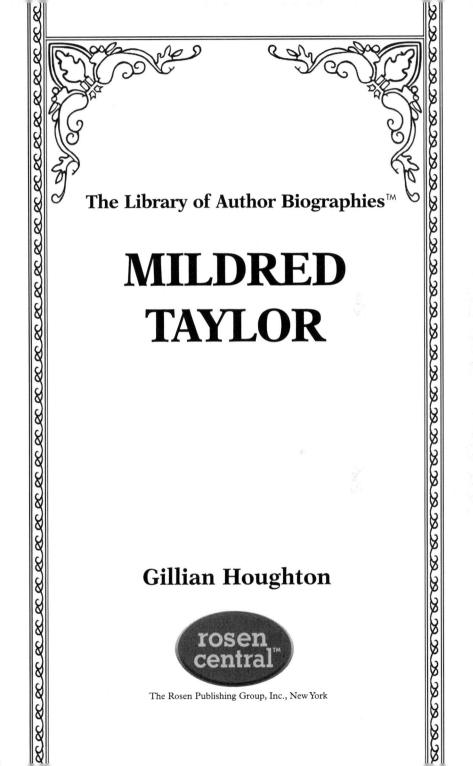

rosen
central™

The Rosen Publishing Group, Inc., New York

Published in 2005 by The Rosen Publishing Group, Inc.
29 East 21st Street, New York, NY 10010

First Edition

Library of Congress Cataloging-in-Publication Data

Houghton, Gillian.
Mildred Taylor/Gillian Houghton.— 1st ed.
    p. cm.—(The library of author biographies)
Includes bibliographical references (p.) and index.
ISBN 1-4042-0330-3 (lib. bdg.)
1. Taylor, Mildred D. 2. Authors, American—20th century—Biography. 3. African American authors—Biography. 4. Americans—Ethiopia—Biography. 5. Ohio—Biography. I. Title. II. Series.
PS3570.A9463Z68 2004
813'.54—dc22

                                                    2004012879

Manufactured in the United States of America

Table of Contents

Introduction

On September 13, 1943, Mildred Delois Taylor was born in her parents' modest home on Everett Street in Jackson, Mississippi. Taylor, who is known to members of her immediate family as Delois, is the second daughter of Wilbert Lee and Deletha Marie Davis Taylor. Mildred's older sister, Wilma, had been born three years earlier.

The baby born that September day would go on to enjoy an accomplished career, to serve overseas as a Peace Corps volunteer, to win the most prestigious awards in the field of young adult literature, and to become a favorite among readers for her stories about the Logan family of Great Faith, Mississippi. But in a sense, Taylor's story begins several hundred years earlier, with the arrival of the first African slaves on North American soil.

Taylor's African American heritage is an integral part of her personal experience and of her literary creations. The long road traveled by African Americans from enslavement to freedom to the gaining of civil rights serves as the backdrop of each of her novels. In the most general terms, Taylor's stories are about an individual's struggle for dignity and self-respect, the terrible power of ignorance and injustice, the importance of family, and the basic right of every person to be truly free. Yet Taylor addresses these issues in a very specific way. For her characters and for Taylor herself, the root of these struggles is racism. To better understand the anger, frustration, and disappointment of Taylor and her characters, it is essential to first consider their shared history.

1 The African American Experience

Africans accompanied Christopher Columbus on his 1492 voyage to the so-called New World, and Africans joined the expeditions of other European explorers such as Balboa, Ponce de León, and Cortés. However, the first African slaves to reach the North American colonies disembarked on the shores of Jamestown, Virginia, in 1619. They were sold as indentured servants—laborers working under contract for a certain period of time for little if any pay beyond the cost of feeding, clothing, and sheltering them.

Initially, many indentured servants were poor European immigrants eager to escape the overcrowding of European cities. As time passed, white immigrants began to seek more varied economic opportunities in the mid-Atlantic and Southern American colonies. Plague swept through England in 1665, killing many, thereby reducing the pressures of over-population there. As a result of these various developments, fewer whites were reduced to indentured servitude at a time when a greater number of laborers were needed to work on the prosperous farms and in the growing towns of colonial Maryland, Virginia, and soon the Carolinas. For these reasons, the end of the seventeenth century saw the large-scale use of enslaved African labor throughout the North American colonies, from the shops of the North to the fields of the South.

These enslaved Africans were generally from small, rural communities in which loyalties within and between families ran deep. The slave trade tested and severed many of these bonds. Africans at every social level participated in the capture and sale of slaves. Men, women, and children were forced into slavery when natural disasters such as drought, or political upheavals such as the rise of regional kingdoms, threatened the survival or altered the social status of their group. Others were kidnapped by fellow Africans as they went about their daily lives, tending goats in an isolated field or foraging for food away from the group. Still others who became slaves were criminals, troublemakers, or otherwise unpopular members of a community who were essentially banished by their countrymen.

European merchants operated a system of barter that modern historians refer to as the "Triangle Trade," a phrase that describes the three-way route traveled by the merchants and slave traders who crisscrossed the Atlantic Ocean. Molasses from West Indian sugar plantations was brought to the North American colonies, where it was distilled into rum, a strong alcoholic beverage. The rum was then shipped to African trading posts. In Africa, rum and other European commodities were traded for slaves, who then endured the horrific Middle Passage across the Atlantic Ocean to the West Indies. There, slaves who had survived the inhumane conditions aboard ships that had managed to avoid pirate attack, naval warfare, and shipwreck were sold to local plantation owners or to North American slave traders.

Because of the dangers of the high seas, the slave trade was a risky venture but also a thriving one for more than a hundred years. However, it experienced a sharp decline around 1800. This was due in part to the spread of democratic political ideals and the development of a popular antislavery movement in both England and some of the Northern American states. In 1807, the United States outlawed the slave trade but not the institution of slavery itself. Although plantation owners could no longer buy slaves from Africa, they could keep the slaves they had and enslave their children and grandchildren. Slave owners could also trade or buy and sell slaves among themselves.

In 1807, the British government also passed legislation outlawing the purchase or transportation of slaves, and in 1834, it outlawed slaveholding in all of its colonies. France and Portugal soon followed suit. Only the United States and Spain continued to allow the sale and ownership of slaves into the latter half of the nineteenth century.

From Slavery to Freedom

Since the beginning of the transatlantic slave trade in the late sixteenth century, some 13 million Africans were bought or captured, shackled in irons, and sent across the Atlantic Ocean in the dank hulls of merchant ships. Of those, around 600,000 reached the United States, a country founded on the principle of liberty for all. As early as the 1660s, the middle colonies—New York, New Jersey, Pennsylvania, and Delaware—had passed laws defining the explicit rights of slaveholders over their property. In Virginia, it was legal for a slave owner to kill his slave as a form of punishment, yet it was illegal for an owner to free a slave, except under special circumstances. It was illegal for whites and blacks, whether slave or free, to marry one another, and slaves could not legally marry one another. Slaves, and to a growing degree, free blacks as well, could not travel without permission, own property, testify in court against a white person, or gather in groups. These racially based laws, known as the black codes, were adopted across the middle and Southern colonies.

In the Carolinas, laws regarding blacks, who soon significantly outnumbered whites, were even more oppressive and sought to strip African Americans of their humanity. According to a 1696 South Carolina law, African slaves were "of barbarous, wild, savage natures, and such as renders them wholly unqualified to be governed by the laws, customs, and practices of this Province."[1] Even in the mid-Atlantic and New England colonies, where slavery had always played a smaller role than in the South, the law defined blacks, both slave and free, as a lower class, subject to a stricter set of rules.

In the years leading up to and immediately following the signing of the U.S. Constitution in 1787, the newly created Northern states came to champion the ideals of independence and move toward the abolition of the slave trade and the emancipation of slaves. The South, however, was firmly rooted, both economically and culturally, in the institution of slavery and the tradition of racism. Southern planters felt they could not afford to abolish slavery and lose all that free labor. And since many of them felt that blacks were "inferior" beings incapable of assuming the rights and responsibilities that belonged to "superior" white Europeans, they felt it would be wrong and dangerous to offer blacks freedom.

The outbreak of the American Civil War in 1861 would do much to bring the abolitionist movement to the forefront of American political debate, and the Emancipation Proclamation, which President Abraham Lincoln issued in 1862, would do a great deal to change the legal status of slaves in the Confederacy—the body of rebellious Southern states. According to Lincoln's order, the slaves in the Confederate states were now free, though the proclamation would have little practical effect until the Union, or the North, beat the Confederacy and enforced abolition.

The battle against racism, in all of its public and private forms, was far from over, however. When the Civil War came to a formal end in 1865, the South was devastated, both economically and emotionally, leading to a bitterness among whites that often fostered resentment and violence against the newly freed blacks. Powerful plantation owners had gone bankrupt, and great numbers of men and boys had been killed in battle, leaving widows and daughters to survive and rebuild on their own. Many of the major cities of the South had been destroyed by enemy bombardment, and many of the farms had grown wild. The foundation of the Southern economy—enslaved black labor—had crumbled.

Perhaps more powerful than this economic depression were the emotional and social upheavals wrought by the war. The campaign to protect slavery and defend states' rights had suffered a humiliating defeat. The South was divided into military districts occupied by Union troops. Blacks were elected to public office and appointed to judgeships. White Northerners hoping to turn a profit in the rebuilding of the South or enter political office with the help of newly emancipated freedmen arrived in great numbers.

They were called carpetbaggers, so named for their cheap traveling bags made out of carpet scraps, and they were often aided by scalawags— Southerners who joined Northerners and blacks in politics or business. Resentment festered among poor, white Southerners as former slaves married, organized separate churches, and demanded fair labor, usually under the system of sharecropping. A sharecropper farms on rented land and receives a share of the value of his or her crops, with the rest going to the landowner.

Reconstruction

The federal government undertook the task of reviving the South's economy while ensuring the safety and civil rights of some 4 million emancipated slaves. This period is known as Reconstruction (1865–1877). Congress created the Freedmen's Bureau, a federal agency that provided financial aid, health care, and educational opportunities to newly emancipated slaves. It also passed the Fourteenth and Fifteenth Amendments of the Constitution, providing citizenship and equal voting rights to all freedmen.

Despite the growing number of new laws on the books designed to protect blacks, many Southerners openly disobeyed the civil rights amendments and were not often punished for it.

Channeling their growing anger and frustration toward free blacks, whites organized secret societies, such as the Ku Klux Klan, and established a strong political base in the Democratic Party. Race riots were not uncommon, but even more pervasive were acts of violence and terrorism against black individuals and their white allies.

By 1877, the federal government and the Northern public had grown weary of Reconstruction. Union troops were withdrawn from their Southern posts, and the Southern Democrats gained majorities in both state and national government. The South entered a new era of "home rule." Northern politicians would no longer interfere in Southern politics, and Southern blacks would be largely left to fend for themselves without government support and protection.

First on the agenda for white Southerners was the disenfranchisement of blacks, or the taking away of their voting rights. Every Southern state enacted discriminatory voting laws, which required black voters to pass literacy tests, pay poll taxes, demonstrate a history of voting in early elections, or a combination of all three. There were laws dictating the hunting and fishing rights of blacks, laws that viewed petty crimes committed by blacks as felonies to be punished by time served on chain gangs, and laws severely limiting the rights of black sharecroppers. Social custom also imposed the strict segregation of whites and blacks, and violence toward blacks increased dramatically. Between 1889 and 1899, there was an average of 187 lynchings in the South every year. A lynching is an execution—often of an innocent person—performed by an angry mob rather than by representatives of the legal system following a trial and conviction for a violent crime.

Two black political movements gained momentum in response to Southern racism. One, led by Booker T. Washington, promoted assimilation and accommodation. Washington urged blacks to accept discrimination, to avoid political and physical conflict with whites, and to develop basic skills, such as farming and metalworking. Through self-improvement tempered by honest hard work, Washington reasoned, blacks would gradually improve their economic status and thereby win the respect of whites. A second movement, led by W. E. B. Du Bois, advocated resistance. Du Bois believed that Washington's policy of meek accommodation would keep blacks permanently enslaved in a system of white racism. In 1909, Du Bois helped organize the National Association for the Advancement of Colored People (NAACP), which even today is a powerful force in the fight against segregation and discrimination in the areas of housing, education, law, public facilities, voter rights, and employment.

Economic Depression and the Great Migration

As racial tensions simmered in the rural South, a crippling economic depression that affected both black and white farmers took hold, first in the 1890s and then in the 1930s. In the 1890s, the demand for the staples of Southern agricultural production—cotton, sugar, rice, and tobacco—was at an all-time low. The resulting surplus was made worse by the increasing number of Southerners planting these crops. With emancipation, thousands of free blacks began to cultivate land once farmed by a relatively small number of whites.

In 1929, the world market for goods collapsed as the Great Depression took hold. This decadelong economic crisis affected virtually every American. In the South, however, blacks suffered the greatest extremes of poverty. Scarce jobs went to whites first. Even menial jobs traditionally relegated to blacks, such as railroad construction and street cleaning, were snatched up by desperate whites.

As early as 1914, blacks had begun to leave the South in large numbers, seeking the "Promised Land" of economic opportunity and greater freedom in the North. By 1930, almost 2 million Southern blacks had moved north. This large-scale exodus from the poverty and racism of the South is known as the Great Migration. Blacks settled in New York City, Pittsburgh, Baltimore, Chicago, Cleveland, Detroit, and virtually every other Northern city. There they found work, most often in factories, saved money, and established vibrant communities, where a new blend of African tradition, Southern custom, and urban flair gave rise to cultural movements such as the Harlem Renaissance.

Mildred Taylor's American South

Those blacks who remained in the South continued to live under the yoke of white racism until the rise of the civil rights movement in the early 1950s. Southern blacks had few opportunities for economic, educational, or social advancement. They were ruled by the wealthy white landowners, resented by poor white farmers who competed for the same scraps of rented land, and unprotected under the law. This is the suffocating, oppressive world inhabited by the Logans, the semi-fictional family whose triumphs and defeats are described in Mildred Taylor's *Song of the Trees* (1975), *Roll of Thunder, Hear My Cry* (1976), *Let the Circle Be Unbroken* (1981), *The Friendship* (1987), *Mississippi Bridge* (1990), *The Road to Memphis* (1990), *The Well: David's Story* (1995), and *The Land* (2001).

The Logans are part of the struggle, which continues to this day, against prejudice, hateful ignorance, and inequality. Taylor's own story is part of the African American experience in the United States, and her work shares in and partakes of her family's long tradition of standing up for itself, honoring its past, and telling stories.

2 Growing Up Black in Civil Rights–Era America

On an October day in 1943, just three weeks after the birth of his daughter, Mildred Delois, Wilbert Lee Taylor came home from work in a fiery mood. He began packing his things, preparing to leave Jackson and the state of Mississippi for good. He had been involved in a dispute at work and had nearly assaulted a white man. For a black man living in the South in the early half of the twentieth century, such an incident was extremely dangerous. If he were formally accused of attacking a white man, Wilbert could face severe punishment under the racist criminal justice system. Furthermore, the law would offer Wilbert no protection against lynch mobs or other forms of violent retribution and intimidation. Wilbert bought a ticket for a northbound train and left Jackson that same day. His wife, Deletha, and her two small children remained behind in the house on Everett Street.

Life on Dorr Street

Wilbert settled in Toledo, Ohio, and found a job in a factory. In the North, blacks were often forced to take jobs where the working conditions were miserable, such as on assembly lines, in meatpacking houses, and in foundries. Blacks were barred from employment in some industrial fields, and competition for factory jobs was fierce. Two months passed before Wilbert was able to save enough money to bring his wife and daughters to the North. The reunited family stayed with friends who, like the Taylors, had migrated from Mississippi in search of a better life.

Eventually, Wilbert saved enough money to buy the family a home of its own. The two-story, wood-frame house stood on a wide thoroughfare called Dorr Street. As Mildred Taylor writes in her autobiographical novella *The Gold Cadillac* (1987), Dorr Street bustled with activity: "On one corner was a grocery store, a cleaner's, and a gas station. Across the street was a beauty shop and a fish market, and down the street was a bar, another grocery store, the Dixie Theater, the café, and a drugstore. There were always people strolling to or from one of these places . . ."[1] Likewise, the Taylor house was often crowded with visiting relatives. Uncles, aunts, and cousins who had recently arrived from the South filled the spare bedrooms. Their love and affection surrounded young Mildred Taylor, their voices filled every room, and their stories fascinated her.

Traveling South

Though the Taylors, their friends, and their relatives had come to the North in search of greater freedom for themselves and their children, they remained deeply bound to the South. Their personal experiences and their cultural heritage were rooted in the fields, forests, and towns of Mississippi and Alabama. For this reason, the family frequently returned to the South, visiting relatives and friends who had remained there, and experiencing life as blacks in the South still knew it. For Mildred and her sister, Wilma, these trips were grand adventures. In preparation for the journey south,

Taylor writes in *The Gold Cadillac*, her aunts and mother prepared an elaborate picnic basket stuffed with fried chicken, baked hams, cakes, sweet potato pies, potato salad, fruit, coffee, and punch. The picnic basket would rest on the backseat, between Mildred and Wilma, who ate happily during the long drive.

In Mississippi, Mildred spent her days playing barefoot outdoors. In her 1977 Newbery Medal acceptance speech, Taylor described these carefree childhood summer days:

> Life was good then. Running barefoot in the heat of the summer sun, my skin darkening to a soft, umber hue; chasing butterflies in the day, fireflies at night; riding an old mule named Jack and a beautiful mare named Lady; even picking a puff of cotton or two— there seemed no better world. [2]

Taylor spent her nights listening to the adults tell stories. These stories transported Mildred and her young cousins to another time, back to the days when her parents, grandparents, and great-grandparents were themselves children playing barefoot on the same rich land.

In many ways, the South that Mildred experienced during these family trips was not so different from the South of so many years before. In the late 1940s, many Southern blacks still lived in rustic cabins or wood-frame houses without indoor plumbing, electricity, or central heating. Water came from a well, light from the glow of an oil lamp, and heat from a blazing fireplace. Farmers traveled by horse or mule, not car, and they worked long hours tending their cotton fields.

Perhaps more important, the South remained a deeply racist, sharply divided place. Restaurants, hotels, stores, schools, and public facilities were segregated, and many bore signs that read "Colored not allowed." Though the Fourteenth and Fifteenth Amendments to the U.S. Constitution promised equal rights regardless of race, the South followed its own set of rules, which were popularly known as Jim Crow laws. This term describes legislation passed between the end of Reconstruction in 1877, and the rise of the civil rights movement in the 1950s.

Jim Crow was the name of a character in a minstrel show created by Thomas Dartmouth Rice in 1828. A minstrel show is a routine performed by white actors in blackface, or wearing dark makeup. The performers tell jokes, sing songs, and act out short comedies that present offensive caricatures of black culture. "Jim Crow" became popular slang for African Americans and synonymous with segregation. Jim Crow laws segregated theaters, cemeteries, schools, parks, public restrooms, restaurants, and even water fountains in an effort to keep whites and blacks entirely separate from one another. The lavish picnic the Taylor family enjoyed during the drive south, Mildred eventually discovered, was not a choice but a necessity forced upon them by Jim Crow segregation. The Taylor family could not stop to eat at the white restaurants along the way. They made the journey without stopping to sleep, because the Taylor family could not stay in the white roadside motels. They traveled in caravans with relatives, because there was greater safety in numbers.

During their trips to Mississippi throughout the 1940s and well into the 1950s, the Taylors were second-class citizens, denied the many rights they enjoyed a few hundred miles north in Toledo, Ohio, and confronted with the prejudices of many white Southerners. Like her parents before her, Mildred came to both love and fear the South. It was a place of great natural beauty, where her family had a proud history and deep roots. But it was also a place of great social ills, where her family could not live in true freedom, security, or safety.

High School, College, and Beyond

In 1953, Wilbert, Deletha, Wilma, and Mildred Taylor moved from their house on Dorr Street to a larger house in a different neighborhood. The family's new neighborhood and Mildred's new elementary school were predominantly white. The following year, Mildred was the only African American student in her sixth-grade class.

These were turbulent times in the United States, as the civil rights movement gained more widespread support and, in response, violence toward blacks escalated among white holdouts. In 1954, the Supreme Court ruled that segregation in public schools was unconstitutional, overturning the fifty-eight-year-old tradition of "separate but equal" that allowed Southern states to keep whites and blacks apart as long as blacks had access to the same kinds of public facilities that whites did, such as schools, parks, and swimming pools. The court ruled that providing separate (and in reality, often unequal) facilities for blacks was not good enough. From now on, every public facility had to welcome both white and black citizens. The next year, a fourteen-year-old black boy from Chicago named Emmett Till, on a visit to relatives in Mississippi, was lynched after being accused of whistling at a white woman. Later that year, Rosa Parks's arrest for refusing to yield her seat to a white passenger and move to the back of a city bus sparked the Montgomery, Alabama, bus boycott, which eventually forced the end of the practice of segregated public transportation in Alabama.

Driven by the belief that her performance reflected, for better or for worse, her entire race, Mildred was an ambitious student. In 1957, she began high school, where she often found herself to be the only black student in her advanced courses. Scott High School was integrated, and the student body was comprised equally of whites and blacks. However, students were grouped by ability. Black students who had attended less rigorous elementary and junior high schools were at a disadvantage. They were placed in less advanced classes and had little opportunity to improve their standing.

Mildred continued to be a hardworking student, determined to prove her worth and the potential of all black students. She was involved in a variety of extracurricular activities, which included serving as a class officer and an editor for the school newspaper. During her senior year, she was elected to the National Honor Society. She was the only black senior at Scott High School to join the honor society that year. Though Taylor has said that she rarely felt open hostility from her white classmates at Scott High School, her freshman year was marked by some unrest when a black senior girl was elected homecoming queen. A few white students were angered by the outcome of the election, and they became violent. The crisis soon subsided, but the event illustrated the extent to which racism existed even in the North.

The year 1957 was a monumental one in the modern civil rights movement. The Southern Christian Leadership Conference, a group of black civil rights activists, was created, and Martin Luther King Jr., was chosen as its president. That year, Congress passed the first civil rights legislation since 1875, creating a federal commission on civil rights and a division of the Justice Department devoted to civil rights issues.

Also that year, Central High School in Little Rock, Arkansas, was forced to integrate. One thousand federal troops were sent to escort nine black students through the crowds of jeering whites gathered in front of the school. In the late 1950s and early 1960s, civil unrest grew. Sit-ins were staged at lunch counters that would not serve black customers. Black and white "freedom riders" boarded buses together to ride south in order to protest the discriminatory policies of bus companies, while others traveled throughout the South to organize voter registration drives. Some 250,000 people joined the march on Washington in 1963, a massive multiracial rally demanding civil rights for blacks. The following year saw the outbreak of race riots in several American cities, including Harlem, Jersey City, Rochester, Philadelphia, and Chicago.

Mildred Taylor graduated from high school in 1961. The following fall, she enrolled at the University of Toledo, where, at her parents' insistence, she entered the school of education, majoring in English with a minor in history. Taylor dreamed of becoming a writer, but her parents convinced her to pursue a more practical degree. It would be difficult to eke out a career as a novelist, they argued, but there would always be a demand for qualified teachers. When she could, Taylor took creative writing courses.

She often found it difficult to write, however, and her stories usually turned out as bland imitations of great writers from the past, such as Charles Dickens and Jane Austen. "I was trying to emulate a literary form that left my work stiff and unconvincing," Taylor has said. "It was an unnatural style for me."[3] Nevertheless, she persevered and completed her first novel, entitled *Dark People, Dark World*, when she was only nineteen. She received favorable feedback from a publishing house and was asked to rewrite the story as a shorter novella, but Taylor, insulted by the suggestion, abandoned the project. In 1965, Taylor graduated with a degree in education. Just days after graduation, she began her official training for the Peace Corps.

Joining the Peace Corps had been a dream of Taylor's since high school. In 1960, she had attended a speech given by Senator John F. Kennedy, under whose presidential administration the Peace Corps was created in 1961. Peace Corps volunteers serve two-year terms in developing countries, providing aid in the areas of agriculture, education, health care, business, technology, and community development. They live and work alongside residents of their host country, laying the foundations of a better standard of living and fostering goodwill toward the United States.

Mildred Taylor had a thirst for travel and adventure. She had long been interested in exploring Africa, especially Ethiopia, one of only several African nations that had resisted European colonization. Ethiopia is notable for its rugged terrain, its variety of religions and languages (some 100 languages are spoken by its ethnically diverse population), and its rich history.

As her college career drew to a close, Taylor completed the long and involved Peace Corps application process and prepared for what promised to be a life-changing journey. Her parents, however, were not supportive and urged her to reconsider, even going so far as to offer her a new car in return for her promise not to enlist as a volunteer. Africa was far away and very dangerous, her parents argued. Furthermore, as a black woman living in a racist country, Mildred owed no service to her government. Their pleas and arguments were made in vain. Mildred remained determined to go.

Then one evening, Mildred's father had a change of heart. At church that night, a young African man had testified to the important work being done by American missionaries in

Africa. The young man was a medical student in the United States, thanks in part to the educational opportunities made possible by Christian missionary groups. Wilbert Taylor became convinced that his daughter's work in Africa was part of God's plan.

Mildred Taylor began her Peace Corps orientation at the University of Utah in 1965, and then spent three weeks teaching English on a Navajo reservation in Arizona. She was then stationed in Yirga 'Alem, Ethiopia, and taught English at a rural school. The two years she spent on her first trip to Ethiopia were powerfully rewarding and enriching. The people of Yirga 'Alem embraced her, adopting her as their sister, daughter, and mother. To them, she was a member of the family, a descendant of the earliest African slaves finally returning home. To Taylor, Ethiopia and its people were an inspiration. The physical landscape of the country reminded her of the American South, and the culture recalled the Southern traditions the Taylor family cherished. But in Ethiopia there was none of the institutionalized racism Taylor had encountered at home or the resulting feeling of humiliation and inferiority. The proud and determined people of Ethiopia were defenders of a rich cultural heritage, and leaders in the Pan-African movement to throw off European and colonial rule.

Back in the United States

Taylor completed her Peace Corps service in the summer of 1967. She briefly considered remaining in Ethiopia, but in the end, she returned to the United States and to her beloved family. She prepared to apply to graduate school. In the meantime, she took a job as a recruiter for the Peace Corps and was stationed in Chicago but made regular visits to colleges throughout the Midwest in search of likely volunteers. She held the job for eight months before relocating to Maine, where she worked as an instructor at a Peace Corps training facility for three months.

In September 1968, she moved to Boulder, Colorado, and began working toward her master's degree in journalism at the University of Colorado. While studying there, Taylor became involved in the Black Student Alliance, an organization created to foster black pride and promote African American interests on campus, such as compelling the university to enroll greater numbers of minority students. The group worked in conjunction with the black studies program. After she earned her graduate degree in August 1969, Taylor remained on campus to work with the black studies program, developing academic skills programs for the campus's African American students.

A False Start

Several months after receiving her master's in journalism, Mildred Taylor was approached by an editor from *Life* magazine who had read an article she had written about the work being done by the University of Colorado's black studies advocates. The editor asked Taylor to write a piece about the program and its effect on academics and student life at the university. This was a thrilling opportunity. *Life* was the most popular magazine of its day. Through photographs and essays, *Life* magazine told the story of the American experience and introduced Americans to issues of international concern.

Taylor went to work on her essay. When she was done, she gave it to members of the Black Student Alliance for review. She incorporated their changes and suggestions and sent the article to the editor at *Life*. The article was rejected. It was criticized as weak and ineffectual, nothing like the earlier article Taylor had written on the subject. Taylor realized that she must have greater confidence in her writing. Her work must speak strongly, distinctively, and from the heart. It must primarily express her opinions and viewpoints in her own voice. Writing by committee and consensus would never produce a distinguished and unique piece of work.

Disappointed and unsure of what to do next, Taylor returned to Ethiopia in the summer of 1970. She remained in Africa until the following fall, when she returned to Colorado and to the black studies program at the university. The following summer, she moved to Los Angeles, California, determined again to make it as a writer.

3 The Stories of the Logan Family

Mildred Taylor arrived in Los Angeles and immediately began to write. She lived off her savings and, when that ran out, she took a job in an office during the day and wrote at night. She sent countless stories to publishers but received only politely worded rejections in return. Meanwhile, in August 1972, she married Errol Zea-Daly and had a daughter, but the couple would divorce three years later. Taylor cherishes her privacy and never discusses her personal or family life in interviews.

Song of the Trees

In October 1973, Taylor learned about a writing contest being held by the Council on

Interracial Books for Children. The deadline for submissions was a mere three days away. From her collection of rejected manuscripts, Taylor chose one that she thought might be appropriate for the contest, a story she had often heard told by her father about a grove of trees and one white man's efforts to steal it. Taylor spent three days revising the short novel, and in the course of these revisions, she created an entirely new character to narrate the events. The novel, *Song of the Trees*, which would win the African American category of the contest and be published by Dial Books in 1975, would be told from the point of view of young Cassie Logan.

The story is set in 1932, and Cassie Logan is eight years old. Cassie is the only daughter of David and Mary Logan. She has three brothers: Stacey, Christopher-John, and Little Man. The family lives in rural Great Faith, Mississippi, on land purchased by their grandfather, Paul Edward Logan, during Reconstruction. Paul Edward's widow, known as Big Ma, has instilled in her sons and grandchildren a deep attachment to the land as the source of both economic security and family pride.

As landowners, the Logans are unique among both blacks and whites in Great Faith, and they will do anything to protect their cotton fields, forests, and pastures. David Logan, or Papa, works on the railroads in Louisiana to earn extra money to meet the mortgage payments and taxes on the land. During one of Papa's long absences from the Logan home, a white man named Mr. Andersen proposes to pay Big Ma $65 in return for as much lumber as he sees fit to cut from the Logans' lush forests. The trees, Cassie tells us, are

> So old that Indians had once built fires at their feet and had sung happy songs of happy days. So old, they had hidden fleeing black men in the night and listened to their sad tales of a foreign land. In the cold of winter when the ground lay frozen, they had sung their frosty ballads of years gone by. Or on a muggy, sweat-drenched day, their leaves had rippled softly, lazily, like restless green fingers strumming at a guitar, echoing their epic tales.[1]

Yet the trees are not simply relics from the past or passive witnesses to the lives of people long dead. They are the living embodiment of the Logans' attachment to the land, and their song is a testament to the family's strength. Like the Logans, the trees stand tall and strong, and their roots dig down deep into the Mississippi soil.

With thinly veiled threats, Mr. Andersen convinces Big Ma that she has no choice but to accept the terms of the agreement. Eleven-year-old Stacey is sent alone on horseback to bring his father home from Louisiana.

By the time the two return four days later, Mr. Andersen's lumber crews have already cut down countless trees. They are at work in the forest on that fourth day when Papa and Stacey appear. Papa carries a black box, which he announces is wired to explosives scattered across the forest. Unless Mr. Andersen and his men leave at once, Papa will blow up the forest. Mr. Andersen tells Papa he must be bluffing. "'One thing you can't seem to understand, Andersen,' Papa said, 'is that a black man's always gotta be ready to die. And it don't make much difference if I die today or tomorrow. Just as long as I die right.'"[2] Mr. Andersen and his crew scurry away, leaving the fallen trees and the Logan family alone in the silent forest.

Song of the Trees was just the beginning of Mildred Taylor's long involvement with the Logan family. Mildred Taylor has published eight books about them, each adding another episode and another shade of character development and historical background to the Logan saga.

Taylor's second and perhaps most famous book is *Roll of Thunder, Hear My Cry*, which was published in 1976. It was followed by *Let the Circle Be Unbroken* in 1981, and *The Friendship* in 1987. Taylor published two books in 1990, *The Road to Memphis* and *Mississippi Bridge*. *The Well* was published in 1995, and *The Land* was published in 2001.

These books—all featuring members of the multigenerational Logan family—span the course of U.S. history from Paul Edward Logan's arrival in Great Faith in 1877 (described in *The Land*) to Moe Turner's hurried departure from Great Faith after assaulting three white teenagers in 1941 (described in *The Road to Memphis*). In addition, Taylor wrote one short, semiautobiographical work, the 1987 book *The Gold Cadillac*, based on her own experiences as a young girl in the early 1950s. She has described this work as being an extension of the Logan saga.

Roll of Thunder, Hear My Cry

A year after winning the Council on Interracial Books for Children contest, Mildred Taylor published her first full-length novel about the Logan family, *Roll of Thunder, Hear My Cry*. Once again the reader sees the world of Great Faith, Mississippi, through the eyes of Cassie Logan, now aged nine. Much of the novel is devoted to expanding the reader's understanding of the everyday lives of blacks in Great Faith. We accompany the Logan children to the segregated community school, where the textbooks are shabby and outdated hand-me-downs from white schools. We witness the Logans enduring the taunts of white children whose school bus careens down the red dirt road every morning, forcing the Logan children to dive into roadside ditches to avoid being hit. Likewise, we relish Stacey's clever revenge upon them.

We visit the Wallace mercantile store, the market in nearby Strawberry, and the annual revival meeting at the black church (in which church members enthusiastically reaffirm their faith in God). We are awoken in the middle of the night by barking dogs and by the bobbing headlights of mysterious cars, and we are kept awake wondering if hot-tempered Uncle Hammer will get into trouble. We visit the Berry family and see the charred body of Mr. Berry, recently burned by white "night men" as punishment for defending a nephew who was accused of looking at a white woman.

At every turn, Cassie and her brothers are exposed to the harsh realities of their time, the prejudices of others, and the importance of family and of land. As Papa whispers reassuringly to Cassie one cold, winter night, "If you remember nothing else in your whole life, Cassie girl, remember this: We ain't never gonna lose this land."[3]

A single plot line is woven through the entire book. It is the story of Stacey's friend T. J. Avery, a foolish black boy who becomes friends with two white teenagers, R. W. and Melvin Simms. The Averys are sharecroppers who do not enjoy the security or independence of owning their own land. There are eight Avery children, and they run virtually wild. The Simms family, with the exception of one mild-mannered son, Jeremy, is a group of hateful, ignorant, white tenant farmers. They are no better off than the Averys, except that they are white, and are therefore protected by the law and the community.

When R. W. and Melvin convince T. J. to rob a store with them, the results are tragic. The store owner catches the trio in the act, and R. W. and Melvin, their faces hidden behind stockings, fatally beat him to death. R. W. and Melvin blame T. J. for the murder, and a posse of angry whites drags him from his home, lynching ropes in hand. Papa Logan sets off to rescue T. J. from the vengeful white mob and moments later, a tremendous fire breaks out in the Logan cotton fields. The whole community, black and white, bands together to put out the blaze, afraid the fire will spread to the neighboring forest owned by the powerful white landlord, Harlan Granger. A great rainstorm drenches the land, T. J. is taken into the sheriff's custody, and the Logans heave a sigh of relief that only a quarter of their cotton crop has been lost.

As she looks out over the smoldering field, Cassie realizes that her father started the fire intentionally, sacrificing the family's only source of income to save poor, misguided T. J. The implication is that only land and family can offer protection for a black person in a world ruled by whites. T. J., lacking both, is doubly cursed. Taylor draws a powerful connection between life and land in the final lines of the book. Cassie mourns T. J.'s inevitable execution and contrasts T. J.'s death with the land's ability to regenerate itself after the fire:

> I had never liked T. J., but he had always been there, a part of me, a part of my life, just like

the mud and the rain, and I had thought that he always would be. Yet the mud and the rain and the dust would all pass. I knew and understood that. What had happened to T. J. in the night I did not understand, but I knew that it would not pass. And I cried for those things which had happened in the night and would not pass. I cried for T. J. For T. J. and the land.[4]

T. J.'s story was based on a story Wilbert Taylor and his brother, James, told Mildred Taylor in 1974. The title of the book comes from a song Mildred wrote while doing laundry in the basement of her parents' Toledo home.

In 1977, *Roll of Thunder, Hear My Cry* was awarded the Newbery Medal, an award sponsored by the American Library Association and presented to the author of the most remarkable children's book published in the previous year. This award signaled that Taylor—with only her second novel—had joined the ranks of the most beloved and critically acclaimed American children's writers.

Let the Circle Be Unbroken

In her Newbery Medal acceptance speech, Mildred Taylor offered this declaration of her intentions as a writer and of her hopes for the future:

> I will continue the Logans' story with the same life guides that have always been mine, for it is my hope that these books, one of the first chronicles to mirror a black child's hopes and fears from childhood innocence to awareness to bitterness and disillusionment, will one day be instrumental in teaching children of all colors the tremendous influence that Cassie's generation—my father's generation—had in bringing about the great Civil Rights Movement of the fifties and sixties.
>
> Without understanding that generation and what it and the generations before it endured, children of today and of the future cannot understand or cherish the precious rights of equality they now possess, both in the North and in the South. If they can identify with the Logans, who are representative not only of my family but of the many black families who faced adversity and survive, and understand the principles by which they lived, then perhaps they can better understand and respect themselves and others. [5]

Her books, Taylor declares, are intended to give the reader a sense of history and of personal responsibility, to trace the journey from childhood to adulthood, to instill honorable values, and to inspire self-reflection.

Perhaps more so than any of Taylor's other books, *Let the Circle Be Unbroken* is a lesson in American history, the story of a particular moment in the national experience. It is about President Franklin Roosevelt's New Deal—a massive government program designed to save the country from the Great Depression—and its effects on rural Southerners, black and white. The book is filled with events in the lives of the Logans and their neighbors—T. J. Avery's murder trial; the arrival of Mama Logan's half-white, half-black great-niece, Suzella; Stacey's growing attachment to Jacey Peters, a black girl who becomes pregnant with a white man's child; Cassie's friendship with the reclusive Wordell Lee; the hardships Stacey and Moe Turner endure when they run away from home to work on the sugarcane plantations of Louisiana; and Mrs. Lee Annie Lees's decision to try to register to vote.

These events provide life lessons for Cassie and her brothers and friends. Each is accompanied by a loss of innocence mixed with confusion, frustration, and anger. Yet all of these events take place against the backdrop of the New Deal, and for the first time in Taylor's fiction, the reader is invited to consider the world outside of Great Faith, Mississippi.

President Franklin Roosevelt took office in 1933, as the Great Depression entered its fourth year. He promised a "new deal" for the "forgotten man" based on a government that provided both immediate financial relief to unemployed, poor, and hungry Americans, as well as long-term regulation of the country's economy to prevent future catastrophic depressions. He created government agencies, such as the Works Progress Administration (WPA) and the Civilian Conservation Corps (CCC), that were responsible for providing emergency aid and creating temporary and long-term employment through federally funded construction and conservation projects.

The National Recovery Administration (NRA) was created to oversee industry and trade, regulating things such as hourly wages and child labor. The Federal Deposit Insurance Corporation (FDIC) served to stabilize the nation's banking system. The Securities and Exchange Commission (SEC) was empowered to police the stock market. The Tennessee Valley

Authority (TVA) was created to provide electricity and prevent floods over an area that spanned seven states in the Southeast.

Of all of Roosevelt's programs, the one that had the greatest effect on Southern farmers was the creation of the Agricultural Adjustment Administration (AAA). This agency was given the task of raising the prices of major crops, such as cotton, thereby improving the income and standard of living for farmers. The plan was to pay farmers to plant and harvest fewer acres, which would result in smaller supplies and higher crop prices for struggling planters. By 1936, the federal government had paid some $1.5 billion to encourage less planting. As the residents of Great Faith would discover, however, this money rarely reached the hands of share-croppers and tenant farmers, the people most in need of it. Instead, landlords, such as Great Faith's Harlan Granger, pocketed the money, explaining that it would be put toward the farmers' outstanding debts.

The action of *Let the Circle Be Unbroken* begins in 1934, the second year of Roosevelt's New Deal. The Logans are wary of Mr. Farnsworth, the local AAA extension agent, and his promises of higher cotton prices. They refuse to sign a contract with the government, but the sharecroppers and tenant farmers on the nearby plantations have no choice but to do so. Their farms are controlled by the white landlords, who, it is later revealed, plan to cheat the government by accepting the farm subsidies while still planting and harvesting the full acreage of cotton. When the landlords' scheme is discovered, almost every family in Great Faith is forced to destroy some portion of their crop to meet the government's quotas. The sharecroppers and tenant farmers are furious, and, adding fuel to the fire, a union organizer named Morris Wheeler has come to the neighborhood. Wheeler urges the people to join together, black and white, and take their demands to the federal government.

The union begins to take shape. Soon, however, Wheeler's house is burned to the ground, one of his black colleagues is found dead, and Wheeler retreats into hiding. The union appears to be crushed. After several of the landlords order the evictions of dozens of families, however, the people come together once again and stage a massive demonstration on the courthouse steps in the nearby town of Strawberry. Harlan Granger rises to speak to the crowd and tells the gathered whites that a mixed labor union can only lead to a total breakdown of a segregated society. The protesters turn violent, are forcibly dispersed, and return home, forgetting all thoughts of a union.

These events loosely parallel the rise of the integrated Southern Tenant Farmers Union, which was founded in Arkansas. The organization opposed the policies of the AAA, specifically the crop reduction program, and gained a significant following, enrolling some 25,000 members across the South. However, little was done by the federal government to address the concerns of poor sharecroppers and tenant farmers until several powerful white supporters were victims of anti-STFU violence. Even then, relief programs for tenant farmers, such as the Resettlement Administration (RA), were limited. Not until the outbreak of World War II (1939–1945) did the demand for agricultural products equal the supply, leading to a rise in the standard of living for rural Southerners. Change would come, but not before rural and urban blacks and whites faced off in race riots and demonstrations.

In *Let the Circle Be Unbroken*, Stacey and Cassie, and even young Christopher-John and Little Man, learn some hard lessons about the world around them. They are becoming young adults and, day by day, a bit more like their parents. The "circle" represents the strength of the Logan family, its continuity from generation to generation, and the bonds the Logans share with friends and neighbors. The "circle" also stands for the great, unrelenting passage of time. Time turns Cassie from a young, headstrong girl into a thoughtful, increasingly wise young woman. Time turns Stacey from being Cassie's playmate to a working man, but in the end, Cassie discovers that these changes bring her and her brother even closer together. Even the strongest families grow and change, but the values and beliefs they share form a sturdy, permanent foundation for each member's life.

The Gold Cadillac

The Gold Cadillac occupies a unique place in Mildred Taylor's list of published works. It is both a part of the Logan saga and separate from it. The story is set in Toledo, Ohio, in the 1950s, and the events are drawn from Taylor's own experiences. The characters are named after Taylor and the members of her immediate family, yet they are meant to represent members of the Logan family after they have migrated to the

North. The major themes of the Logan family books—a strong sense of family, self-respect in the face of prejudice, and the heritage of Southern racism—are echoed in *The Gold Cadillac*, establishing a strong bond between the two separate narratives.

Wilbert Taylor has bought a brand-new gold Cadillac, a jewel of a car. While his daughters, Mildred and Wilma, his relatives, and his neighbors are in awe of the beautiful automobile, Wilbert's wife, Dee, remains unimpressed. She is angry that Wilbert selfishly bought such an expensive toy when the family was saving for a new home. When Wilbert announces his intention to drive the new car to Mississippi, Dee is convinced it will only bring trouble. However, the whole family decides to accompany Wilbert and his new car to the South.

In Tennessee, just across the border with Mississippi, Wilbert Taylor's gold Cadillac is stopped by the police. The police do not believe Wilbert when he claims the car belongs to him. They put him in the back of their squad car, and one of the policemen gets behind the wheel of the Cadillac. With the patrol car in the lead, the two cars head into the nearest town, where Wilbert is detained at the police station for three hours. Wilbert is finally released, and the family continues to drive south in the gold Cadillac.

After a frightening night spent sleeping in the car, Wilbert turns the Cadillac around and returns north. In Memphis, he leaves the Cadillac at a cousin's house and borrows the cousin's less conspicuous Chevrolet. Wilbert, Dee, Wilma, and Mildred drive the Chevrolet to Mississippi without incident and enjoy a brief visit with family there. Back in Toledo, Wilbert sells the Cadillac, convinced that the car is trouble and that the world is not ready to accept a black man in a shiny new gold Cadillac. Taylor ends the book with this passage:

> After that we drove around in an old 1930s Model A Ford my father had. He said he'd factory-ordered us another Mercury, this time with my mother's approval. Despite that, most folks on the block figured we had fallen on hard times after such a splashy showing of good times and some folks even laughed at us as the Ford rattled around the city. I must admit that at first I was pretty much embarrassed to be riding around in that old Ford after the splendor of the Cadillac. But my father said to hold my head high. We and the family knew the truth. As fine as the Cadillac had been, he said, it had pulled us apart for a

while. Now, as ragged and noisy as that old Ford was, we all rode in it together and were a family again. So I held my head high.

Still though, I thought often of that Cadillac. We had had the Cadillac only a little more than a month, but I wouldn't soon forget its splendor or how I'd felt riding around inside it. I wouldn't soon forget either the ride we had taken south in it. I wouldn't soon forget the signs, the policemen, or my fear. I would remember that ride and the gold Cadillac all my life. [6]

The Gold Cadillac offers a rare glimpse into Mildred Taylor's personal history. The reader comes to know an eager, precocious girl named 'lois, her loving relatives, and her committed parents. Dorr Street is brought to life, as is the Taylor house. For the first time, we are given young Mildred's firsthand account of her reactions to segregation and prejudice—the terrible fear, the confusion, and the anger that it excites in her. As the book's final passage indicates, the drive south in the gold Cadillac was a critical event in young Mildred's life. Its importance to Taylor becomes even more clear when one considers that this is the only story taken directly from her own experience that she has published. Drawn from the events of her childhood, *The Gold Cadillac* directly reflects Taylor's values and beliefs. By extension, the reader is asked to reconsider all of Taylor's books in this light, as living illustrations of the principles with which she was raised.

The Friendship and *Mississippi Bridge*

The Friendship and *Mississippi Bridge* describe two brief yet powerful events that each takes place over the course of a single day in Great Faith, Mississippi. Instead of focusing on the action and its impact on Cassie and the rest of the Logan family, these novellas highlight the struggles of other characters within the Great Faith community. The reader discovers, perhaps more so than in any other Taylor book, that the hurt and anger felt by the Logans are shared by other black, and even white, residents. Similarly, the strength and integrity the Logans exhibit can be found in other families, too.

The Friendship is narrated by nine-year-old Cassie, but the story belongs to Mr. Tom Bee. Bee is an elderly black man who, on two occasions many years ago, saved the life of a white man named John Wallace, owner of the Wallace mercantile store. In recognition of Mr. Tom Bee's kind treatment, John Wallace had promised that for the rest of his life, Bee could refer to Wallace by his first name. This was very rare. Whereas whites of any age could refer to a black man or woman by any name or derogatory term they wished—including disrespectfully addressing an elderly black man as "boy"—blacks were forbidden to call a white man or woman by his or her first name only.

For example, a teenage Melvin Simms, who is white, is free to call Papa Logan "David" or even "Boy," but Papa Logan must say "Mr. Melvin" in response. This custom had little to do with demanding politeness and respect. Many whites wanted to humiliate blacks and treat them as servants or inferior, infantile creatures, so they demanded to be addressed with humility and respect, while offering degrading treatment in return.

One day, Cassie and her brothers meet Mr. Tom Bee at the Wallace store and agree to wait for him before continuing on their walk. While the children linger on the front porch, they over-hear Wallace's two grown sons, Dewberry and Thurston, refuse to serve Bee. They grow angry when the elderly black man demands to speak to their father, calling John Wallace by his first name. Wallace appears, sends his sons out of the store, and speaks in strained tones to Bee, demanding that Bee refer to him in the customary way. "Ain't necessarily what I'm wanting," John Wallace says, "but what's gotta be. You just can't keep going 'round callin' me by my first name no more. Folks been taking note. Makes me look bad. Even my boys been questionin' me on why I lets ya do it . . . I'm losin' face, Tom." Tom Bee refuses to give in, reminding Wallace of the service he rendered him: "Now, what you think I care 'bout your face, boy? I done saved your hide more'n one time and I gots me a right t' call you whatsoever I pleases t' call you whensoever I be talkin' t' ya!"[7]

Wallace fills Bee's order of sardines and penny candy, and Bee turns to leave. He gathers up the children on the front porch, and the group walks to a nearby neighbor's house to deliver medicine before turning back toward home. Along the way, they must pass the Wallace store once again, and Tom Bee announces that he forgot to buy some tobacco. Again, Bee leaves the children outside and enters the store, where the Wallaces have been joined by the Simms brothers, R. W. and Melvin, and their father, Charlie. In front of the gathered whites, Bee again calls Wallace by his first name. The room grows quiet, and Wallace passes the tobacco across the counter. Bee turns and leaves the store, but John Wallace is just behind him. The blast of a shotgun sounds, and Bee falls on the ground in front of the porch, shot in the leg. Wallace and the other white men appear on the porch and issue a severe warning, but Bee will not be intimidated.

Looking down the barrel of Wallace's shotgun, Mr. Tom Bee lets loose a torrent of anger and frustration, shouting at John Wallace that he will never back down. Bee's fiery, defiant, and moving words call to mind Papa Logan's speech in *Song of the Trees*, in which he declares that every black man must always be prepared to die. *The Friendship* ends there. Bee's fierce speech needs no other explanation or comment; it is the very embodiment of awe-inspiring courage and self-respect.

Mississippi Bridge is narrated by Jeremy Simms, the quiet, thoughtful brother of racist and violent R. W. and Melvin Simms, the two boys who betray T. J. Avery after a botched store robbery in *Roll of Thunder, Hear My Cry*, and witness the shooting of Mr. Tom Bee in *The Friendship*. While spending a rainy afternoon on the front porch of the Wallace store, Jeremy watches a group of people, both black and white, gather to meet the bus headed north to Jackson, Mississippi. First comes a black teenager named Rudine Johnson and her mother. A white woman, Miz Hattie McElroy, soon follows with her four-year-old grand-daughter, Grace Anne. Then Jeremy sees Josias Williams approach the store in his best Sunday clothes. Josias, a black teenager and a friend of Jeremy's, tells Jeremy that he is on his way to see about a job with a lumber crew on the Natchez Trace (an eighteenth-century wilderness road connecting the lower Mississippi River to Central Tennessee. But when Jeremy's father, Charlie Simms, who is in the Wallace store with Jeremy's brothers, overhears Josias boasting about the prospect of a job, he becomes incensed. He corners Josias, demanding to know whether he thinks he is better than the scores of white men, like himself and his sons, who cannot find work. Josias struggles to save himself from Charlie Simms's wrath, finally claiming that he had been lying about the job.

Humiliated and angry, Josias leaves the store to wait on the porch, alongside Jeremy, who feels miserable for not defending his friend against his father. Finally, Big Ma Logan arrives with her grandchildren in tow, and soon the bus pulls up in front of the store. Rudine and her mother, Miz Hattie, Grace Anne, Josias, and Big Ma board the bus. The Logan children are sent home, and, for a while, Jeremy follows them, eager as always to be their friend. Just before the bus leaves, a large white family arrives and prepares to board the bus. There is not enough room, and the driver forces all of the black passengers to get off to make room. The bus barrels away, leaving Rudine, her mother, Josias, and Big Ma in the rain.

The rain is relentless, and a thick fog settles in. On its way out of town, the bus skids on the rotten planks of an old bridge, veers off the road, and falls into the raging river below. Jeremy is the only witness, but Josias soon reaches the scene of the accident, as do the Simmses and the Wallaces. The bodies of Miz Hattie and the other white passengers are recovered from the wreck, but everyone on board the bus has been killed. The black travelers left behind have been spared, thanks to the prejudice of the bus driver and the system of segregation prevalent throughout the South.

Mississippi Bridge is, like all of Taylor's books, a story about racism and its impact on the lives of the blacks of Great Faith. Perhaps more important, however, it is a story about

Jeremy Simms and the conflict he experiences between his own beliefs and values, and those of the white society that raised him and to which he belongs. Jeremy looks on with shame as John Wallace first refuses to let Rudine Johnson try on a hat in the store, then flatters Miz Hattie as she tries on the same hat. He cringes when he sees the anger and humiliation in Josias's eyes after his encounter with Jeremy's father.

Jeremy is eager to befriend the Logan children, but his attempts are politely rebuked. He is heartbroken to see Josias lift the limp bodies of Miz Hattie and Grace Anne from the river. They are not hateful racists like Jeremy's father, but nevertheless Miz Hattie and Grace Anne are participating members of an unjust society, as is Jeremy himself. Jeremy is helpless to defend his black friends against the prejudice of his family and neighbors, and the heavy weight of guilt and loneliness he bears as a result threatens to crush him.

In her acceptance speech for the 1997 ALAN (Assembly on Literature for Adolescents of the National Council of Teachers of English) Award, Mildred Taylor said, "In the writing of my books I have tried to present not only a history of my family, but the effect of racism, not only to the victims of racism but to the racists themselves."[8] The white passengers aboard the bus in *Mississippi Bridge* are implicated in the racist society in which they live, and they seem to receive a sort of cosmic punishment when they plunge into the river.

When Taylor discusses the effects of racism on racists, however, she is talking about more than this kind of twist of fate that brings a story to a neat, ironic close. Taylor sees racism as a festering sore on the skin, eating away at healthy cells. It corrupts the young and sours the old. Blind hate erupts in violence, and violence becomes second nature. The bonds of family and friendship grow weak. *In Mississippi Bridge*, Jeremy says of his father:

> One time I seen Pa and Melvin and R. W. and a whole bunch drag a colored man down the road, beat him till he ain't hardly had no face on him 'cause he done stood up for himself and talked back. That ain't never set right with me, the way Pa done. It wasn't right and I just know'd it, but I ain't never let Pa know how I was feeling, 'cause Pa he could get awful riled and riled quick. Last thing a body wanted to do, blood or not, was to get on Pa's wrong side. You got on Pa's wrong side and you done had it. [9]

Because he recognizes the injustice of racism, Jeremy becomes another kind of victim of it. Like Wade Jamison, the white defense attorney who ably but unsuccessfully defends T. J. during his murder trial in *Let the Circle Be Unbroken*, Jeremy is ostracized, or shunned, by both whites and blacks. Whites see him as someone who has an unnatural regard for blacks, and blacks have come to learn that more often than not, nothing but trouble can come from friendship with whites. In a racist society, there is no place for Jeremy's genuine understanding and compassion.

4 The Big Ideas

All of Mildred Taylor's books reflect the importance the Taylor family placed on the strength of the bonds its members shared and on the independence blacks could hope to gain and preserve by owning property. The family is the main source of love, creative power, comfort, sympathy, and inspiration. From her father, Taylor inherited the ability, desire, and sense of obligation to share her family stories. She writes in the author's note to *Roll of Thunder, Hear My Cry*:

> My father was a master storyteller. He could tell a fine old story that made me hold my sides with rolling laughter and

sent happy tears down my cheeks, or a story of stark reality that made me shiver and be grateful for my own warm, secure surroundings . . .

By the fireside in our northern home or in the South where I was born, I learned a history not then written in books but one passed from generation to generation on the steps of moonlit porches and beside dying fires in one-room houses . . . From my father the storyteller I learned to respect the past, to respect my own heritage and myself. From my father the man I learned even more, for he was endowed with a special grace that made him tower above other men. [1]

Mildred Taylor's stories are drawn from these same tales she heard by firesides and on front porches, and her characters are often modeled on members of her family. In dedicating *Roll of Thunder* to her father, recently deceased when the book was published in 1976, Taylor writes, "To the memory of my beloved father who lived many of the adventures of the boy Stacey and who was in essence the man David."[2] The character of David's brother Hammer was largely taken from two of Taylor's great-uncles, and David's wife, Mary, was based on Taylor's grandmother.

Christopher-John and Little Man Logan are based on two of Taylor's uncles, and Cassie is a mixture of her Aunt Sadie, her sister, Wilma, and Mildred Taylor herself.

Both the Taylors and the Logans understand that as long as they were dependent on the whims of white landlords, they would not be free or safe. The land, whether it is the Logans' sprawling 400 acres or the Taylors' lot and house on Dorr Street, provides stability and instills personal pride. In *Let the Circle Be Unbroken*, Cassie tells a character named Dubé Cross the story of Paul Edward Logan's purchase of the land in the Reconstruction era. The story has a profound and inspiring effect on the stuttering Cross:

> Dubé shook his head, impressed. "One of th-these here d-d-days, gonna have myself a place. Nice p-p-place like th-this of m-my own." His eyes swept the land. "Y-y-y'all some kkkk-kinda lucky." [3]

The Logans are unique among their neighbors because they have land. Many of their white neighbors do not even own their own land or houses. According to Taylor, the Logans are also unique among modern representations of black families, because the Logans are committed to each other and to their beliefs. In this way, they diverge from the stereotypes set forth in most books, films, and television programs about African Americans, which present young blacks as urban, uneducated children of broken homes, cared for by single mothers and burdened by poverty, crime, drugs, and other urban ills. Taylor wanted to offer an alternate and healthier model of African American life by presenting a black family that enjoyed both financial security and love. She also wanted to introduce readers to an African American culture and history left out of the textbooks she encountered as a child.

In her acceptance speech for the *Boston Globe*/Horn Book Award, which she won for *The Friendship*, Taylor describes her elementary and high school history classes:

> [C]lasses devoted to the history of black people in the United States always caused me painful embarrassment. This was because history had not been presented truly, showing the accomplishments of blacks both in Africa and in this hemisphere. But, as it was, as the textbooks and the teachers presented the history, the indictment of slavery was

also an indictment of the people who were enslaved—a people who, according to the texts, were docile and childlike, accepting their fate without once attempting to free themselves. To me this lackluster history of black people, totally devoid of any heroic or pride-building qualities, was as much a condemnation of myself as it was of my ancestors. I used to sit tensely waiting out those class hours trying to think of ways to repudiate what the textbooks said, for I recognized that there was a terrible contradiction between what was in them and what I learned at home.[4]

Black history, as narrated by Taylor's white teachers, was not only inaccurate, but also uninspiring. It filled Taylor with none of the heart-thumping wonder that her father's stories evoked. The African Americans she learned about in school never displayed their courage by standing up to their oppressors, like Mr. Tom Bee had, or demanding their rights, like Mrs. Lee Annie Lees, or by simply living a moral life, like Mama and Papa Logan. Taylor saw it as her obligation, both to her immediate family and to all African Americans, to present a true, proud image of blacks in the United States. Her efforts have been praised and rewarded, and her devoted readers are the wiser for having walked a few miles in the Logans' shoes.

Happily, that journey with the Logans is not yet at an end. Mildred Taylor, who today lives in Colorado, continues to work on the Logan family saga.

Conclusion

Mildred Taylor has earned the most prestigious honors bestowed on writers of young adult fiction. In 1974, she won first prize in the African American category of the annual Council on Interracial Books for Children contest. When *Song of the Trees* was published two years later, it was chosen as a *New York Times* Outstanding Book of the Year, a Coretta Scott King Honor Book, and a Jane Addams Honor Book. In 1977, *Roll of Thunder, Hear My Cry* was awarded the Newbery Medal and was chosen as a finalist for the National Book Award. It was also chosen as an American Library Association Notable

Book, a Young Reader's Choice book, and a *Boston Globe*/Horn Book Fiction Honor Book, among almost a dozen other honors. Her books were honored with the Coretta Scott King Award (honoring one outstanding African American author each year), for *Let the Circle Be Unbroken*, *The Friendship*, *The Road to Memphis*, and *The Land*. Both *The Gold Cadillac* and *Mississippi Bridge* were honored with the Christopher Award. *The Well: David's Story* earned ten awards or citations for excellence in children's literature.

Critical praise has greeted the publication of each of her books. Reviews often cite the poetic style Taylor employs to describe the natural world, the vibrant characterizations of Great Faith's residents, the richly woven narrative threads, and the powerful effect on the reader of Taylor's examination of racism. Yet some critics find her depictions of racist beliefs and behaviors to be almost too brutal in their honesty. Taylor recounted in a 2001 interview with *Booklist* that when *Roll of Thunder, Hear My Cry* first appeared in 1976, some white parents contended that the scenes of racism described in the book were too extreme and outlandish to be true. Twenty-five years later,

Taylor faced criticism from black parents for presenting the harsh realities of the black experience in America. In her *Booklist* interview, Taylor described their reactions to *The Land* and defended her work, saying:

> Now the same thing is going on with black families who don't want their children to hear the "n" word and to hear about the truth. How can I tell a story about this period in our history without using this word? Without talking about the racist views and the way people were treated then? Some black parents don't even want their children to know that black people were second-class citizens in the past and that they had to react in a certain way just to survive. Well, why was there a civil rights movement, and what is the meaning of the Martin Luther King holiday? [1]

Mildred Taylor's books are modern classics of young adult literature, though her readership is by no means confined to teenagers. Reading any one of the Logan family stories is a memorable experience for any reader, and many of Taylor's most loyal and enthusiastic fans are grown-ups who first encountered her books twenty years ago. A reader of Mildred Taylor's novels is not likely to forget the way his or her heart sank when T. J. Avery was found guilty of murder or the way it surged with pride and righteousness when Mr. Tom Bee railed against John Wallace. These events, and many others, have carved out a place in our child-hoods, forever occupied by Mildred Taylor.

Interview with Mildred Taylor

The *Booklist* Interview (September 15, 2001)

In a rare interview, her first in many years, Mildred Taylor spoke with *Booklist* from her home in Colorado about her latest novel, *The Land*, and how it fits with her other books about the Logan family, including her acclaimed Newbery Award winner, *Roll of Thunder, Hear My Cry* (1976). In *The Land* (which received a starred Focus review in the August 2001 issue of *Booklist*), Taylor goes back to the time of Reconstruction to tell a searing story of cruelty, racism, and betrayal. It's also a thrilling coming-of-age story of friendship, hope, and family strength. Paul-Edward tells it in his own voice: born of a part Indian, part African slave mother and a white plantation-owner father and raised by both his parents, his dream is to own his own land.

BOOKLIST: In your 1977 Newbery acceptance speech, you talk about how painful it was for you as a child in history classes to see the way that black people were portrayed or left out altogether. Has the teaching of history changed?

TAYLOR: Oh, definitely. It's no longer just history from the European point of view. I get many letters from schools, including from those where the majority of students are white, and the children tell me they read *Roll of Thunder* along with other books about U.S. history. Children today are so much more aware of what life must have been like 40 years ago or a century ago, and they have a much greater respect for the contributions African Americans have made to this country. When I was a child, I would never have known about that from history books. I learned the history from my family.

BOOKLIST: You've always said that your books draw directly on your own family history. How much is that true of *The Land*? Is Paul-Edward based on your great-grandfather?

TAYLOR: I've always been fascinated by my great-grandfather and his story: that he came out of slavery, that he felt allegiance to both sides of his family, that he grew throughout this whole experience and was able to get his own land. All the people in my family, especially my father, were always passing these stories on. Even as a child, I sat there and listened. And, for whatever reason, I was given this need to put these stories on paper, as if I were the one who was tapped by God. Family gatherings and storytelling are where all my stories come from.

BOOKLIST: I just can't forget that scene when the white farmer tears up the land contract he signed with Paul-Edward. Is that a true story?

TAYLOR: Yes. The man reneged on his deal and took back the land after my great-grandfather had cleared it.

BOOKLIST: And did his white father also teach him the bitter lesson that touching a white man in anger might cause him to be lynched?

TAYLOR: From all the stories I've heard, this was just one of the things he learned from his father. His father gave him an education and treated him almost as an equal to his brothers. My great-grandfather learned from his father and also from his mother. That's one thing I was hoping to show: that within this one person, there were three heritages, African, British, and Native American. It was such a central part of America during those days to have a part of each of these continents within one person.

BOOKLIST: You also show clearly how much he suffered because of his race. It's right there in the author's note on the very first page, where you say that you refuse to whitewash history, that "the language was painful and life was painful for many African Americans, including my family." How do you feel about those who want to ban your books because you use the "n" word and show the suffering?

TAYLOR: As a parent, I do understand people trying to protect their children from pain. What I do not understand is denying their children their heritage. I am concerned that people don't want their children to hear the truth. When *Roll of Thunder* first came out 25 years ago, there were white families who criticized it, saying, "Oh, this would never have happened." And, of course, it had happened. Now the same thing is going on with black families who don't want their children to hear the "n" word and to hear about the truth. How can I tell a story about this period in our history without using this word? Without talking about the racist views and the way people were treated then?

Some black parents don't even want their children to know that black people were second-class citizens in the past and that they had to react in a certain way just to survive. Well, why was there a civil rights movement, and what is the meaning of the Martin Luther King holiday? I mean, yes, we have equal rights, or so-called equal rights today. We have so many more opportunities. Children of all races and cultures and backgrounds have the opportunity to advance in this country now. It's amazing how much has changed. But I think each of us needs to know where America was in the past, where we came from—not just African Americans, but Hispanics and Asians and Native Americans. It's about all of us.

BOOKLIST: In the foreword to the 25th anniversary edition of *Roll of Thunder*, published this year, you talk about your own childhood before the civil rights movement and what it was like being faced with segregation and bigotry.

TAYLOR: I remember how it was. I remember being told that we couldn't use the restroom. I remember store clerks saying, "Oh, you can't try those clothes on." I remember some very racist statements—just like those of some of the characters in *Roll of Thunder* and *The Land*—and I remember being terrified as a child when I came across people like that. What I have always tried to do in my books is to have the reader walk in the shoes of my characters. And I guess I've done a relatively good job as a writer if people get upset because they have had to walk in the shoes of this family. If they had to go down into a segregated South, as I did as a child, they would know that what I show is the truth.

BOOKLIST: Are you going to write more about the Logan family?

TAYLOR: The last book will take the Logan children, all grown up, through the end of World

War II, the years following, and then the beginning of the civil rights movement. For the first time, I'll have to weave a part of my own life into the story.

—*Interview conducted by Hazel Rochman*

Timeline

September 13, 1943 Mildred Delois Taylor is born in Jackson, Mississippi.

October 1943 Wilbert Taylor moves to Toledo, Ohio. Two months later, his wife and daughters join him.

1953 Wilbert, Deletha, Wilma, and Mildred Taylor move to a newly integrated Toledo neighborhood.

1957 Mildred Taylor attends Scott High School in Toledo.

1961 Taylor graduates from Scott High School and enrolls at the University of Toledo.

1962 Taylor writes her first novel, *Dark People, Dark World*, which is never published.

1965 Taylor graduates from the University of Toledo with a bachelor's degree in education, with a major in English and a minor in history.

1965–1967 Taylor works as an English teacher in Ethiopia, serving as a member of the Peace Corps.

1967–1968 After returning to the United States, Taylor works as a Peace Corps recruiter and then as an instructor before enrolling in the Graduate School of Journalism at the University of Colorado in September 1968.

1969 Taylor graduates with a master's degree in journalism but stays on at the University of Colorado working with the black studies program.

1970 Taylor spends the summer in Ethiopia while considering her career and life goals.

1971 Taylor moves to Los Angeles, California, where she works in an office during the day and writes at night.

August 1972 Taylor marries Errol Zea-Daly. The couple will have a daughter but be divorced in 1975.

1974 Taylor wins the African American category of the Council on Interracial Books for Children contest. Her winning story will be published the following year as *Song of the Trees*.

1976 Wilbert Taylor dies. Mildred Taylor publishes *Roll of Thunder, Hear My Cry*.

1977 Taylor is awarded the Newbery Medal for *Roll of Thunder, Hear My Cry*.

1981 Taylor publishes *Let the Circle Be Unbroken*.

1987 Taylor publishes *The Gold Cadillac* and *The Friendship*.

1990 Taylor publishes *The Road to Memphis* and *Mississippi Bridge*.

1995 Taylor publishes *The Well: David's Story*.

2001 Taylor publishes *The Land*.

Selected Reviews from *School Library Journal*

The Friendship
1987

Grades 2–6—A hot, humid afternoon in Mississippi in 1933 is the setting for a tense drama and tragic confrontation between Mr. Tom Bee, an elderly black man, and a white store owner, John Wallace. The interaction between the two men portrays how severely the bonds of friendship can be tested against a backdrop of racism, peer pressure, and individual rights. This novella is narrated by Cassie Logan from *Roll of Thunder, Hear My Cry* (Dial, 1976). She and her brothers go to the country store for some medicine for a neighbor. At the store, they are hassled by Wallace's sons. They run into Mr. Bee, who addresses John Wallace by his first name. Blacks are forbidden to do so, but Mr. Bee had saved John's life on more than one occasion, and John had given him permission to call him by his first name. Under pressure and taunting by the men in his store, John reneges on his promise in an explosive and devastating outburst. The characterization is very strong in this brief drama, and the events of this fateful afternoon will be unforgettable. The black-and-white illustrations are noteworthy, and depict the story's mood and action well. This book lends itself well to discussions on various topics pertaining to human relations.

The Gold Cadillac

1987

Grades 2–3—In this quiet story, 'lois explains a child's perspective of her fears when she, her sister Wilma, and their parents drive from Ohio to visit relatives in Mississippi in 1950. When 'lois' father buys a new gold Cadillac, his wife refuses to ride in it until he declares his intentions to visit his parents in the South. Then the whole family goes, caravan style, for it's "a mighty dangerous thing, for a black man to drive an expensive car into the rural South."

'lois and Wilma are disquieted by the increasing appearance of "white only, colored not allowed" signs as they drive further south. After white policemen humiliate and arrest their father, they do visit their grandparents, but the trip results in their father giving up the car when they return home, realizing that it was pulling the family apart. Full-page sepia paintings effectively portray the characters, setting, and mood of the story events as Hays ably demonstrates his understanding of the social and emotional environments which existed for blacks during this period. 'lois' first-person narrative allows readers to understand the youthful perspective on the dehumanizing intentions of racism. Clear language and logical, dramatic sequencing of story events make this story bittersweet for adult readers but important for the social development of beginning readers.

Mississippi Bridge
1990

Grades 5–10—Drawing once again upon her father's stories, Taylor has created a harsh, disturbing tale of racism in Mississippi during the 1930s. Told from the viewpoint of Jeremy

Simms, a ten-year-old white boy who aspires to be friends with the black children of the Logan family, this is the story of a rainy day, an overloaded bus, and the destiny of its passengers after the driver has ordered the black travelers off to make room for latecoming whites. Telescoping the injustices faced by blacks on a daily basis into one afternoon drives home the omnipresent effects of racism with a relentless force. This is an angry book, replete with examples of the insults and injuries to which the African-American characters are subjected. Jeremy, the only white character to acknowledge this unfairness, is brought to task by his father for "snivelin'" after the Logans. The book's climax is a catastrophic accident in which the bus crashes off a bridge, killing the passengers. When Jeremy asks a black rescuer how such a thing could happen, he is told, "the Lord works in mysterious ways." This is a disturbing explanation, not for its implication that the white passengers are being punished for the sins of their race so much as for the logical extension that the black characters were saved because they were kept off the bus in the first place. Well written and thought provoking, this book will haunt readers and generate much discussion.

The Well: David's Story

1995

Grades 4–6—Another contribution to the Logan family saga, this is Father's account of an incident from his boyhood. During a drought in 1910, 10-year-old David Logan's family has the only working well in their part of Mississippi. They share their water willingly with both black and white neighbors, but white teenager Charlie Simms tests their generosity, goading David's older brother Hammer into a fight requiring restitution in the form of labor on the Simms's farm. Charlie and his brother get even for the disgrace of Hammer's beating by secretly contaminating the Logans' well with dead animals, only to be exposed and punished when a neighbor reveals their act. While David narrates, this is really Hammer's story; his pride and steely determination not to be put down are the source of the novel's action and power. Readers will feel the Logans' fear and righteous anger at the injustice and humiliation they suffer because they are black. As in *The Friendship* (Dial, 1987), Taylor has used her gift for storytelling and skillful characterization to craft a brief but compelling novel about prejudice and the saving power of human dignity.

The Land

2001

Grades 7–10—In this prequel to *Roll of Thunder, Hear My Cry* (Dial, 1976), readers meet the relatives of the Logan family who lived during Civil War and Reconstruction times. Paul Edward is the son of a slave and her white master. He is treated well by his white half brothers and by his father, who teaches him to read and write. However, he and his sister learn that they are part of the white family in only certain respects. Early in his life, Paul is tormented for his mixed racial heritage by a black boy, Mitchell Thomas, who later becomes his best friend. The story follows these two young men as circumstances force them to run away from home and make their way in the world. Through hard work, the kindly help of a white employer, and sheer determination, Paul logs a tract of land that will supposedly be his. After much backbreaking labor, he is cheated out of it by the white owner. The plot takes several surprising twists as Paul and Mitchell fall in love with the same young woman, and tragedy lies in wait for them. The ugliness of racial hatred and bigotry is clearly demonstrated throughout the book. The characters are crisply drawn and believable, although at times Paul's total honesty, forthrightness, and devotion to hard work seem almost too good to be true. While this book gives insight and background to the family saga, it stands on its own merits. It is wonderful historical fiction about a shameful part of America's past. Its length and use of the vernacular will discourage casual readers, but those who stick with it will be richly rewarded. For fans of the other Logan books, it is not to be missed.

List of Selected Works

Song of the Trees. New York: Dial Press, 1975.

Roll of Thunder, Hear My Cry. New York: Dial Press, 1976.

Let the Circle Be Unbroken. New York: Dial Press, 1981.

The Friendship. New York: Dial Books for Young Readers, 1987.

The Gold Cadillac. New York: Dial Books for Young Readers, 1987.

Mississippi Bridge. New York: Dial Books for Young Readers, 1990.

The Road to Memphis. New York: Dial Books, 1990.

The Well: David's Story. New York: Dial Books for Young Readers, 1995.

The Land. New York: Phyllis Fogelman Books, 2001.

List of Selected Awards

The ALAN (Assembly on Literature for
Adolescents of the National Coucil of
Teachers of English) Award (1997)
Neustadt Prize for Children's Literature (2003)

***Song of the Trees* (1975)**
Coretta Scott King Honor Book
Council on Interracial Books for
Children Award
Jane Addams Honor Book
New York Times Outstanding Book of
the Year

***Roll of Thunder, Hear My Cry* (1976)**
American Library Association (ALA)
Notable Book

American Book Award
Boston Globe/Horn Book Fiction Honor Book
Buxtehuder Book Award
Coretta Scott King Honor Book
Jane Addams Honor Book
National Book Award finalist
Newbery Award
New York Times Best Books for Children and
    Young Adults
Young Reader's Choice

Let the Circle Be Unbroken (1981)
ALA Best Books for Young Adults
ALA Notable Book
American Book Award Finalist
Coretta Scott King Award
Jane Addams Honor Book
New York Times Outstanding Book

The Friendship (1987)
Boston Globe/Horn Book Award
Coretta Scott King Award

The Gold Cadillac (1987)
Christopher Award
New York Times Notable Book

Mississippi Bridge (1990)
Christopher Award
Jane Addams Honor Book

The Road to Memphis (1990)
ALA Notable Book
Best Book for Young Adults
Coretta Scott King Award

The Well: David's Story (1995)
ALA Notable Book
American Bookseller Pick of the Lists
Jane Addams Award
New York Public Library's 100 Titles for
    Reading and Sharing
New York Public Library's Books for the Teen Age

The Land (2001)
Coretta Scott King Award

Glossary

accommodation The act of adapting or resigning oneself to the ideals or attitudes of a given, usually dominant, group.

assimilation The process of being absorbed into a culture, society, or group and adopting its characteristics and values.

abolition The formal act of putting an end to slavery.

banished Forced to leave a country or a place.

bankrupt A state of financial ruin or poverty.

black codes Laws promoting the segregation of the races.

carpetbaggers Northerners who went south after the Civil War to seek economic opportunity or political office with the help and support of newly freed slaves.

civil rights The rights of personal liberty guaranteed to U.S. citizens by the Thirteenth and Fourteenth Amendments to the Constitution (which abolished slavery and granted citizenship and civil liberties to freed slaves) and by acts of Congress.

Confederacy The eleven Southern states that seceded from the United States in 1860 and 1861, leading to the American Civil War.

disembarked Having gone to shore from a ship.

disenfranchisement Having a legal right—such as the right to vote—taken away.

emancipation The act of being freed from restraint, control, or the power of another person, government, or institution.

emulate To strive to be like, to imitate.

explicit Fully and clearly expressed, with no opportunity for misunderstanding.

ignorance A state in which one lacks knowledge, education, or understanding.

indentured To be bound by a contract.

integral Essential to the completeness of something.

lynch mobs Groups of people who seize and punish others without relying on the legal system and its courts. Lynch mobs in the American South often executed black victims by hanging. Many of these victims were entirely innocent of any crime and hanged simply because of the color of their skin.

migration The movement of a large group of people from one place to another.

missionaries People who are sent to do religious or charitable work, usually in a foreign country.

oppressive Unreasonably severe and harsh.

Peace Corps An agency of the federal government that is devoted to world peace and friendship and helping individuals build a better life for themselves, their children, and their communities. Peace Corps Volunteers are invited by host countries to work on issues ranging from AIDS education, information technology, business development, and environmental preservation.

plague An epidemic disease that causes many deaths.

prestigious Honored; having high standing or influence.

race riots A large public disturbance caused by racial tension or anger.

racism The belief that race accounts for differences in ability or character, and that one race is superior to another.

Reconstruction The period immediately following the Civil War when the rebellious Southern states that had seceded from the Union were controlled by the federal government before being readmitted into the Union.

scalawags White Southerners working for or supporting the federal government during Reconstruction.

segregation The separation or isolation of a class, race, or ethnic group through housing and education policies, social barriers, and other forms of formal and informal discrimination.

Union The states that remained in the federal union during the American Civil War.

For More Information

Web Sites

Due to the changing nature of Internet links, the Rosen Publishing Group, Inc., has developed an online list of Web sites related to the subject of this book. This site is updated regularly. Please use this link to access the list:

http://www.rosenlinks.com/lab/mita

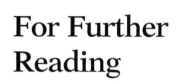

For Further Reading

Browne, Ray B., and Lawrence A. Kreiser Jr. *The Civil War and Reconstruction.* Westport, CT: Greenwood Press, 2003.

Candaele, Kerry. *Bound for Glory: From the Great Migration to the Harlem Renaissance, 1910–1930.* Langhorne, PA: Chelsea House Publishers, 1997.

Chafe, William, Raymond Gavins, Robert Korstad, and the staff of the Behind the Veil Project, eds. *Remembering Jim Crow: African Americans Tell About Life in the Segregated South.* New York: New Press, 2003.

Davidson, Margaret. *I Have a Dream: The Story of Martin Luther King.* New York: Scholastic, 1994.

Finlayson, Reggie. *We Shall Overcome: The History of the American Civil Rights Movement*. New York: Lerner Publishing Group, 2002.

Hansen, Joyce. *"Bury Me Not in a Land of Slaves": African-Americans in the Time of Reconstruction*. New York: Franklin Watts, 2000.

Levine, Ellen. *Freedom's Children: Young Civil Rights Activists Tell Their Own Stories*. New York: Putnam Publishing Group, 2000.

Parks, Rosa, and James Haskins. *Rosa Parks: My Story*. New York: Puffin Books, 1999.

Patterson, James T. *Brown v. Board of Education: A Civil Rights Milestone and Its Troubled Legacy*. New York: Oxford University Press, 2002.

Williams, Juan. *Eyes on the Prize: America's Civil Rights Years, 1954–1965*. New York: Penguin Books, 1988.

Wormser, Richard. *The Rise and Fall of Jim Crow*. New York: St. Martin's Press, 2003.

Ziff, Marsha. *Reconstruction Following the Civil War*. Berkeley Heights, NJ: Enslow Publishers, 1999.

Bibliography

Crowe, Chris. *Presenting Mildred D. Taylor.* New York: Twayne Publishers, 1999.

Jenkins, Wilbert L. *Climbing up to Glory: A Short History of African Americans During the Civil War and Reconstruction.* Wilmington, DE: Scholarly Resources, Inc., 2002.

Rochman, Hazel. "The *Booklist* Interview: Mildred Taylor." *Booklist.* September 15, 2001. Retrieved May 2004 (http://archive.ala.org/booklist/v98/se2/69interview.html).

Scott, William R., and William G. Shade, eds. *Upon These Shores: Themes in the African-American Experience, 1600 to the Present.* New York: Routledge, 2000.

Taylor, Mildred. "Acceptance of the *Boston Globe*/Horn Book Award for *The Friendship*," *Horn Book Magazine* 65, no. 2 (March/April 1989): pp. 179–80.

Taylor, Mildred. "Acceptance Speech for the 1997 ALAN Award," *ALAN Review* 25 (spring 1998): p. 3.

Taylor, Mildred. *The Friendship*. New York: Puffin, 1998.

Taylor, Mildred. *The Gold Cadillac*. New York: Puffin, 1998.

Taylor, Mildred. *Let the Circle Be Unbroken*. New York: Puffin, 2002.

Taylor, Mildred. "Mildred Taylor," in *Something About the Author: Autobiography Series*, vol. 5, Adele Sarkissianed, ed. Detroit, MI: Gale Research, 1988: p. 268.

Taylor, Mildred. *Mississippi Bridge*. New York: Puffin, 2000.

Taylor, Mildred. "Newbery Medal Acceptance," *Horn Book Magazine* 53, no. 4 (August 1977): p. 403.

Taylor, Mildred. *Roll of Thunder, Hear My Cry*. New York: Puffin, 2002.

Taylor, Mildred. *Song of the Trees*. New York: Puffin, 2003.

Source Notes

Chapter 1

1. William R. Scott and William G. Shade, eds., *Upon These Shores: Themes in the African-American Experience, 1600 to the Present* (New York: Routledge, 2000), p. 78.

Chapter 2

1. Mildred Taylor, *The Gold Cadillac* (New York: Puffin, 1998), p. 22.
2. Mildred Taylor, "Mildred Taylor," *Something About the Author: Autobiography Series*, Vol. 5, Adele Sarkissian, ed. (Detroit, MI: Gale Research, 1988), p. 268.
3. Ibid.

Chapter 3

1. Mildred Taylor, *Song of the Trees* (New York: Puffin, 2003), pp. 33–34.
2. Ibid., pp. 43–44.
3. Mildred Taylor, *Roll of Thunder, Hear My Cry* (New York: Puffin, 2002), p. 152.
4. Ibid., p. 276.
5. Mildred Taylor, "Newbery Medal Acceptance," *Horn Book Magazine*, Vol. 53, No. 4 (August 1977): p. 403.
6. Mildred Taylor, *The Gold Cadillac* (New York: Puffin, 1998), pp. 41–43.
7. Mildred Taylor, *The Friendship* (New York: Puffin, 1998), pp. 31–32.
8. Chris Crowe, *Presenting Mildred D. Taylor* (New York: Twayne Publishers, 1999), p. 49.
9. Mildred Taylor, *Mississippi Bridge* (New York: Puffin, 2000), p. 21.

Chapter 4

1. Mildred Taylor, *Roll of Thunder, Hear My Cry* (New York: Puffin, 2002), author's note.
2. Ibid., author's dedication.
3. Mildred Taylor, *Let the Circle Be Unbroken* (New York: Puffin, 2002), p. 129.
4. Chris Crowe, *Presenting Mildred D. Taylor* (New York: Twayne Publishers, 1999), p. 119.

Conclusion

1. Rochman, Hazel. "The *Booklist* Interview: Mildred Taylor." *Booklist*. September 15, 2001. Retrieved May 2004 (http://archive.ala.org/ booklist/v98/se2/69interview.html).

Index

About the Author
Gillian Houghton is a freelance writer living in Chicago, Illinois.

Photo Credits
Cover, p. 2 photo courtesy of Nancy Jacobs

Designer: Tahara Anderson